US NATIONAL PARKS

ALASKA

☐ Glacier Bay
☐ Katmai
☐ Kenai Fjords
☐ Lake Clark
☐ Wrangell – St. Elias
☐ Denali
☐ Kobuk Valley
☐ Gates of the Arctic

AMERICAN SAMOA

☐ American Samoa

ARIZONA

☐ Saguaro
☐ Petrified Forest
☐ Grand Canyon

ARKANSAS

☐ Hot Springs

CALIFORNIA

☐ Death Valley
☐ Channel Islands
☐ Joshua Tree
☐ Kings Canyon
☐ Lassen Volcanic
☐ Pinnacles
☐ Redwood
☐ Sequoia
☐ Yosemite

COLORADO

☐ Mesa Verde
☐ Great Sand Dunes
☐ Black Canyon of the Gunnison
☐ Rocky Mountains

FLORIDA

☐ Biscayne
☐ Dry Tortugas
☐ Everglades

HAWAII

☐ Hawaii Volcanoes
☐ Haleakalā

INDIANA

☐ Indiana Dunes

KENTUCKY

☐ Mammoth Cave

MAINE

☐ Acadia

MICHIGAN

☐ Isle Royale

MINNESOTA

☐ Voyageurs

MISSOURI

☐ Gateway Arch

MONTANA

☐ Glacier

NEVADA

☐ Great Basin

NEW MEXICO

☐ Carlsbad Caverns
☐ White Sands

NORTH DAKOTA

☐ Theodore Roosevelt

OHIO

☐ Cuyahoga Valley

OREGON

☐ Crater Lake

SOUTH CAROLINA

☐ Congaree

SOUTH DAKOTA

☐ Wind Cave
☐ Badlands

TENNESSEE

☐ Great Smoky Mountains
(Also in NC)

TEXAS

☐ Big Bend
☐ Guadalupe Mountains

U.S. VIRGIN ISLANDS

☐ Virgin Islands

UTAH

☐ Zion
☐ Bryce Canyon
☐ Canyonlands
☐ Capitol Reef
☐ Arches

VIRGINIA

☐ Shenandoah

WASHINGTON

☐ Mount Rainier
☐ North Cascades
☐ Olympic

WEST VIRGINIA

☐ New River Gorge

WYOMING

☐ Grand Teton
☐ Yellowstone

CANADIAN NATIONAL PARKS

ALBERTA

- ☐ Wood Buffalo
- ☐ Waterton Lakes
- ☐ Banff
- ☐ Jasper
- ☐ Elk Island

BRITISH COLUMBIA

- ☐ Pacific Rim
- ☐ Gulf Islands
- ☐ Kootenay
- ☐ Mount Revelstoke
- ☐ Glacier
- ☐ Yoho
- ☐ Gwaii Haanas

MANITOBA

- ☐ Riding Mountain
- ☐ Wapusk

NEW BRUNSWICK

- ☐ Fundy
- ☐ Kouchibouguac

NEWFOUNDLAND AND LABRADOR

- ☐ Terra Nova
- ☐ Gros Morne
- ☐ Mealy Mountains
- ☐ Torngat Mountains

NORTHWEST TERRITORIES

- ☐ Nahanni
- ☐ Nááts'ihch'oh
- ☐ Thaidene Nëné
- ☐ Tuktut Nogait
- ☐ Aulavik

NOVA SCOTIA

- ☐ Sable Island
- ☐ Kejimkujik
- ☐ Cape Breton Highlands

NUNAVUT

- ☐ Ukkusiksalik
- ☐ Auyuittuq
- ☐ Sirmilik
- ☐ Qausuittuq
- ☐ Quttinirpaaq

ONTARIO

- ☐ Point Pelee
- ☐ Rouge
- ☐ Thousand Islands
- ☐ Georgian Bay Islands
- ☐ Bruce Peninsula
- ☐ Pukaskwa

PRINCE EDWARD ISLAND

- ☐ Prince Edward Island

QUEBEC

- ☐ La Mauricie
- ☐ Forillon
- ☐ Mingan Archipelago

SASKATCHEWAN

- ☐ Grasslands
- ☐ Prince Albert

YUKON

- ☐ Kluane
- ☐ Vuntut
- ☐ Ivvavik

Visas

Visas

Visas

Visas

Visas

Visas

Visas

Visas

Visas

Visas

Visas

Visas

Visas

Visas

Visas

Visas

Visas

Visas

Visas

Visas

Visas

Visas

Visas

Visas

Visas

Visas

Visas

Visas

Visas

Visas

Visas

Visas

Visas

Visas

Visas

Visas

Visas

Visas

Visas

Visas

Visas

Visas

Visas

Visas

Visas

Visas

Visas

Visas

Visas

Visas

Visas

Visas

Visas

Visas

Visas

Visas

Visas

Visas

Visas

Visas

Visas

Visas

Visas

Visas

Visas

Visas

Visas

Visas

Visas

Visas

Visas

Visas

Visas

Visas

Visas

Visas

Visas

Visas

Visas

Visas

www.ingramcontent.com/pod-product-compliance
Lightning Source LLC
Chambersburg PA
CBHW041326110526
44592CB00021B/2838

* 9 7 8 1 9 2 7 9 7 7 5 5 2 *